lonely planet **KIDS**

THE BIG BOOK OF

AIRPLANE

ACTIVITIES

WRITTEN BY LAURA BAKER
ILLUSTRATED BY SOPHIE FOSTER

TIME TO FLY!

SOLVE THE CLUES AND FILL IN THE CROSSWORD.

During take-off, flaps on a plane's wings are raised to help it lift.

ACROSS
4. The part of an airplane that helps it stay balanced
5. The place you go to catch a flight
6. A document you need to travel to a different country
8. A plane has two of these—one on each side
9. The place in an airport where you wait to board a plane

DOWN
1. A bag you use to carry your things when going on a trip
2. A boarding pass is your _ _ _ _ _ _ to travel on a plane
3. The person who flies the airplane
7. The long path where planes take off and land

AT THE AIRPORT

CAN YOU FIND ALL THE WORDS IN THE GRID?

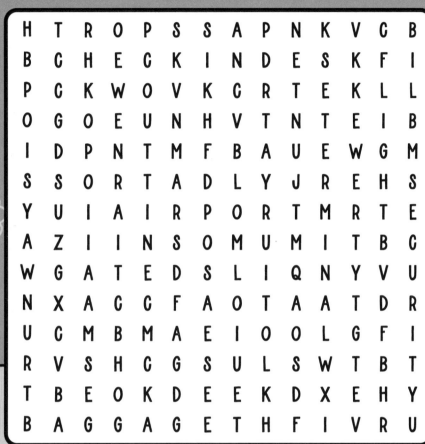

```
H T R O P S S A P N K V C B
B C H E C K I N D E S K F I
P C K W O V K C R T E K L L
O G O E U N H V T N T E I B
I D P N T M F B A U E W G M
S S O R T A D L Y J R E H S
Y U I A I R P O R T M R T E
A Z I I N S O M U M I T B C
W G A T E D S L I Q N Y V U
N X A C F A O T A A T D R
U C M B M A E I O O L G F I
R V S H C G S U L S W T B T
T B E O K D E E K D X E H Y
B A G G A G E T H F I V R U
```

AIRPORT   CONTROL TOWER   PASSPORT   SECURITY

BAGGAGE   FLIGHT   PLANE   SUITCASE

CHECK-IN DESK   GATE   RUNWAY   TERMINAL

The largest plane in the world was designed to carry a space shuttle on its back!

FILL THE SUITCASE

WHAT WOULD YOU PACK FOR AN EXCITING TRIP?
DRAW IT HERE. FILL THE SUITCASE WITH YOUR MUST-HAVE ITEMS.

CASTING SHADOWS

WHICH AIRPLANE IS CASTING THE SHADOW ON THE GROUND?

Not all planes carry people. Cargo planes carry goods such as food, clothes, machines, and more to places all around the world.

PACK YOUR BAGS

THESE ARE ALL THINGS YOU MIGHT NEED TO TAKE WITH
YOU ON A FLIGHT. CAN YOU FIT THEM IN THE GRID?
LOOK CAREFULLY AT THE NUMBER OF LETTERS TO HELP YOU.

The first
suitcase with
wheels attached
was invented
in 1970.

5 LETTERS
WATER

8 LETTERS
MAGAZINE
PASSPORT

9 LETTERS
SANITIZER

10 LETTERS
HEADPHONES
SUNGLASSES

12 LETTERS
BOARDING PASS
TRAVEL PILLOW

ISLAND GETAWAY

WHICH AIRPLANE IS HEADING TO THIS TROPICAL ISLAND?
FOLLOW THE PATHS TO FIND OUT.

St. Helena, an island in the middle of the South Atlantic Ocean, is so remote that planes only started flying there a few years ago.

AT THE GATE

CAN YOU SPOT THESE ITEMS AT THE GATE?
CHECK THEM OFF AS YOU GO.

- [ ] TEDDY
- [ ] GREEN SHOES
- [ ] WATER BOTTLE
- [ ] YELLOW AIRPLANE
- [ ] STAR
- [ ] NEWSPAPER

The largest passenger plane in the world is the Airbus A380. It has 16 doors, 220 windows, and can carry more than 500 people.

DEPARTURES

Time	Destination	Gate
8:35	ATLANTA	NOW BOARDING
9:00	DUBAI	NOW BOARDING
9:20	HONOLULU	DELAYED
9:45	KIEV	GO TO GATE 7
0:05	NAIROBI	11
0:30	AUCKLAND	2
0:55	BARCELONA	18

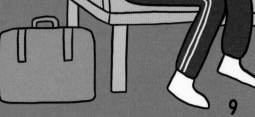

- ☐ TOILET SIGN
- ☐ TWO COFFEE CUPS
- ☐ CLOCK
- ☐ RAINBOW LUGGAGE TAG
- ☐ WINDSOCK
- ☐ WATCH

DREAM HOLIDAY

IF YOU COULD FLY ANYWHERE IN THE WORLD, WHERE WOULD YOU GO? SKETCH YOUR DREAM DESTINATION HERE.

A-Z SPOTTING

WHAT CAN YOU SPOT WHEN YOU'RE ON A FLIGHT?
TRY TO THINK OF SOMETHING FOR EVERY LETTER OF
THE ALPHABET. BE AS CREATIVE AS YOU CAN!

The first-ever
non-stop flight across
the Atlantic Ocean
happened in 1919.
It took more than
16 hours.

Airplane	N
B	O
C	P
D	Q
E	R
F	S
G	T
H	U
I	V
J	W
K	X
L	Y
M	Z

PLANE PAIR

LOOK CLOSELY AT ALL THE AIRCRAFT IN THE BUSY SKY.
WHICH TWO ARE EXACTLY THE SAME?

When not in use, airplanes park in huge garages called hangers.

SAYING HELLO

THERE ARE DIFFERENT WAYS TO SAY "HELLO" IN DIFFERENT PLACES. MATCH EACH PHRASE WITH THE LANGUAGE IT IS FROM.

OLÁ

CIAO

HALLO

Some experts believe human language began with signs and gestures before developing into vocal sounds.

NǏ HǍO

NAMASTE

BONJOUR

LANGUAGES

CHINESE   HINDI
DUTCH   ITALIAN
FRENCH   PORTUGUESE

SECURITY SCRAMBLE

HOW MANY WORDS CAN YOU MAKE FROM THE LETTERS IN THE WORD "SECURITY"? WHAT'S THE LONGEST WORD YOU CAN MAKE?

SECURITY

UNIDENTIFIED LUGGAGE

CONNECT THE DOTS TO DISCOVER WHAT IS
TRAVELING ALONG THE BAGGAGE CAROUSEL.

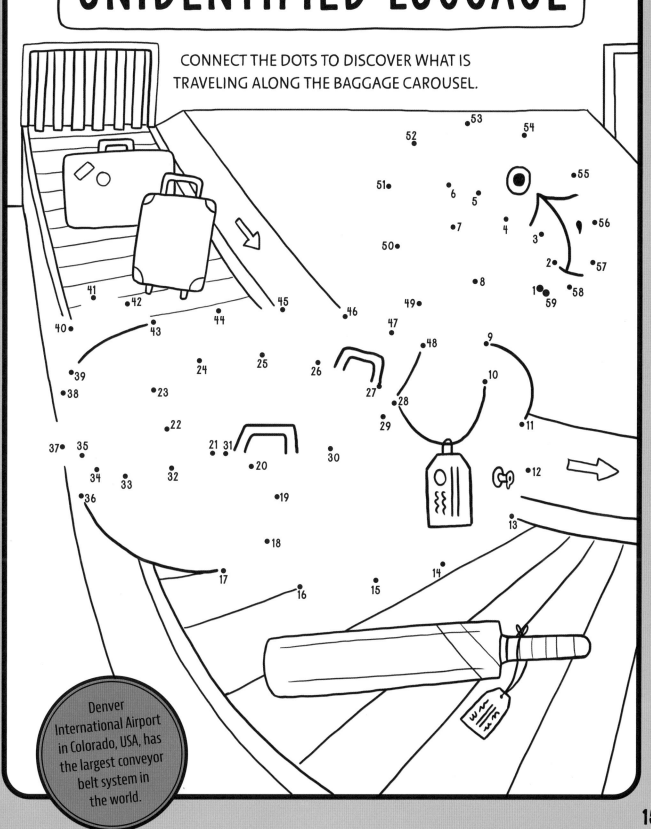

Denver International Airport in Colorado, USA, has the largest conveyor belt system in the world.

IN THE CLOUDS

FILL IN THE GRIDS SO THAT EACH ROW, COLUMN, AND SECTION CONTAINS
ALL THE LETTERS OF THE WORD ABOVE THE GRID.

BIRD

B			D
		B	
I			B
	B	I	R

LAND

L			N
N		L	
			L
D	L		A

Artist and inventor Leonardo da Vinci built a flying machine based on how birds and bats fly.

AIRPLANE GIGGLES

DRAW LINES TO MATCH EACH JOKE TO ITS PUNCHLINE.

Luggage is moved from the terminal to the aircraft on trailers attached to baggage trucks.

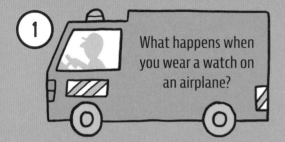

1 What happens when you wear a watch on an airplane?

2 What has a nose but can't smell?

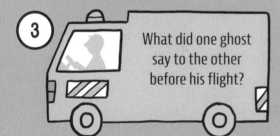

3 What did one ghost say to the other before his flight?

4 How do rabbits travel so fast?

5 What do you get when you cross an airplane and a magician?

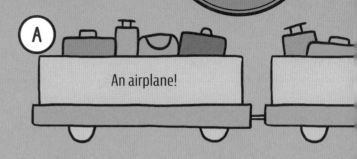

A An airplane!

B They have private HARE-planes!

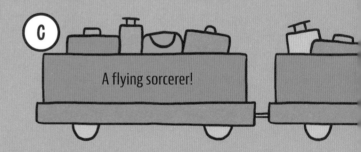

C A flying sorcerer!

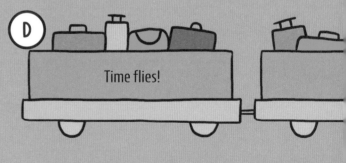

D Time flies!

E "Have a good fright!"

TAKE-OFF

COLOR IN THIS PICTURE USING THE KEY.

The part of a plane where luggage is stored is called the cargo hold. It is located under the aircraft.

1 = YELLOW 2 = RED 3 = GREEN 4 = GREY 5 = BLUE

SIGN SYMBOLS

SOLVE THE PROBLEMS TO FIGURE OUT THE CODE.
THEN ANSWER THE QUESTION BELOW.

(A) $4 + 7 =$ ___

(B) $20 - 6 =$ ___

(D) $11 - 8 =$ ___

(E) $11 - 10 =$ ___

(G) $10 + 10 =$ ___

(I) $12 - 10 =$ ___

(M) $11 + 5 =$ ___

(N) $18 - 3 =$ ___

(O) $9 + 9 =$ ___

(R) $3 + 6 =$ ___

(W) $12 - 5 =$ ___

(Y) $2 + 2 =$ ___

What is the message on the board at the gate?

PASSENGER INFORMATION

Flight 182:

15 18 7
□ □ □

14 18 11 9 3 2 15 20
□ □ □ □ □ □ □ □

The first
successful aircraft
flight traveled just
37 m (120 feet).

19

BOARDING PASS MATCH

MATCH THE BOARDING PASSES TO MAKE PAIRS.
CAN YOU FIND WHICH PASS IS FOR A ONE-WAY FLIGHT ONLY?

FROM: LONDON
TO: NEW YORK
SEAT: 17C

SEAT: 8F
FROM: DOH...
TO: MIAMI

SEAT: 28B
FROM: CAIRO
TO: LIMA

FROM: CHICAGO
TO: HOUSTON
SEAT: 2A

FROM: JOHANNESBURG
TO: CAPE TOWN
SEAT: 12E

SEAT: 4F
FROM: PERTH
TO: TOKYO

SEAT: 33D

FROM: LIMA
TO: CAIRO
SEAT: 11B

FROM: FRANKFURT
TO: DUBLIN
SEAT: 33C

FROM: DUBLIN
TO: FRANKFURT
SEAT: 26A

FROM: CAPE TOWN
TO: JOHANNESBURG
SEAT: 30A

FROM: HOUSTON
TO: CHICAGO
SEAT: 32C

FROM: BRASILIA
TO: PARIS
SEAT: 20E

FROM: HONG KONG
TO: BEIJING
SEAT: 14F

FROM: PARIS
TO: BRASILIA

FROM: MIAMI
TO: DOHA
SEAT: 29D

FROM: NEW YORK
TO: LONDON
SEAT: 22B

FROM: BEIJING
TO: HONG KONG
SEAT: 23D

The world's longest direct flight goes from New York to Singapore. It takes just under 19 hours.

21

GOING-AWAY GIFT

FIND AND CIRCLE THE 10 DIFFERENCES BETWEEN THESE TWO PICTURES.

BON VOYAGE

UNCOVER THE HIDDEN MESSAGE BY CRACKING THE CODE BELOW.

An aircraft called the Solar Impulse 2 was the first plane to fly around the world on solar power (energy from the Sun).

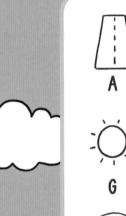

A   B   D   E   F

G   H   I   L   M

O   R   S   T   V

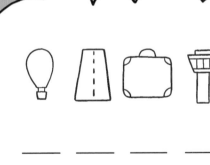

_____

 !

_____

FRIENDLY FLYERS

WHO IS FLYING ON THIS AIRPLANE?
SKETCH FACES ONTO THE PASSENGERS.

Some airplanes that fly long distances have secret bedrooms where the crew can rest.

BOARD GAMES

LOOK CLOSELY AT THE ARRIVALS AND DEPARTURES BOARDS SHOWING FLIGHTS COMING INTO AND GOING FROM THIS INTERNATIONAL AIRPORT. THEN ANSWER THE QUESTIONS BELOW.

ARRIVALS

Time	Arriving from	Gate	Expected
10:05	SHANGHAI	12	ARRIVED
10:15	NEW YORK	4	ARRIVED
10:27	PARIS	17	DELAYED
10:38	ROME	7	ON TIME
11:00	SAN FRANCISCO	8	CANCELLED
11:18	CHICAGO	2	ON TIME
11:30	MILAN	17	ON TIME

1
I am waiting for my friend to arrive from New York. Has she landed yet?
_____

2
My brother's plane has arrived at gate 12. Where is he flying from?
_____

3
My mother is traveling from Rome. She wants to catch a connecting flight to New York. Will she make it?
_____

4
Which arriving flight is delayed?
_____

DEPARTURES

Time	Destination	Gate	Expected
10:00	BOSTON	17	BOARDING
10:11	LONDON	3	GO TO GATE
10:30	TOKYO	5	GO TO GATE
10:46	DUBAI	6	GO TO GATE
11:05	ISTANBUL	2	CANCELLED
11:10	MIAMI	17	DELAYED
11:45	NEW YORK	4	ON TIME

The world's shortest international flight is just eight minutes long. It goes between the Caribbean islands of Anguilla and Sint Maarten.

5 Which departing flight is canceled?
_____

6 Which gate has the most flights coming and going?
_____

7 I need to fly to London. Which gate should I go to?
_____

8 Which plane is boarding right now?
_____

COMING IN TO LAND

GUIDE THE AIRPLANE THROUGH THE CLOUDS
TO MAKE A SAFE LANDING AT THE AIRPORT.

START

FINISH

Some special planes do tricks in the air during airshows. The tricks are called "aerobatics."

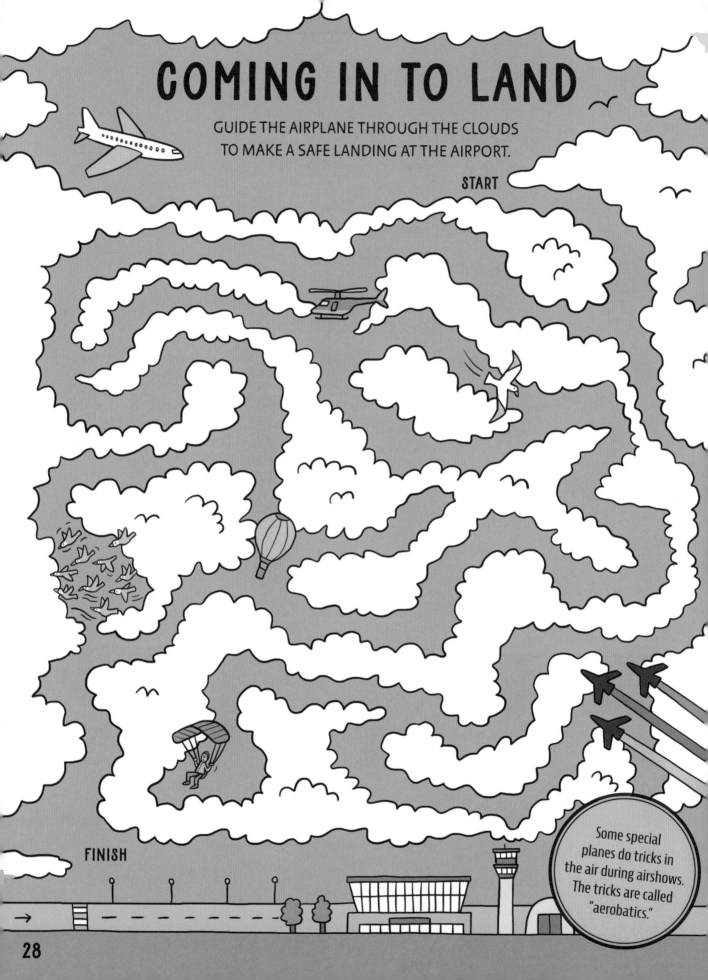

COUNTRY SEARCH

CAN YOU FIND ALL THE WORDS IN THE GRID?

```
D G I C E L A N D C T V E K
E S B G W J Y N U R Q R J U
A S U D A N A S D G O N L K
P B O A U Y T M R P W L K R
B N E I C A S D A F G H J A
M G C L X Z W G E I R T Y I
O H U A G Y N D G L C J K N
V A B R W I C V N E P A L E
W N V T S M U X K T Y U I O
H A J S L Z I M B A B W E R
U Q B U V T N A T N M U T Y
C R E A F I N L A N D S H M
P M E X I C O T M B C U B A
X S C P W Y C A U V J C R I
```

AUSTRALIA   ICELAND   PERU

BELGIUM   JAMAICA   SINGAPORE

CUBA   MALTA   SUDAN

FINLAND   MEXICO   UKRAINE

GHANA   NEPAL   ZIMBABWE

Nepal is the only country that doesn't have a square or rectangular flag.

MIXED-UP PARTS

UNSCRAMBLE THESE WORDS TO UNCOVER DIFFERENT PARTS OF AN AIRPLANE. USE THE CLUES TO HELP YOU.

1. The machine that powers the plane: IEGENN _ _ _ _ _ _

2. The flat pieces that stick out on each side to help the plane fly: NSIGW _ _ _ _ _

3. The front end of the plane: ENSO _ _ _ _ _

4. The rear part of the plane: ALIT _ _ _ _ _

5. The place where suitcases and cargo are stored: ODHL _ _ _ _ _

The spinning paddles on the front or sides of a plane are called propellers. They help lift the aircraft and move it forward.

UNDER CONTROL

CONNECT THE DOTS TO UNCOVER THE TALL BUILDING
WHERE WORKERS MANAGE AIR TRAFFIC.

Air traffic controllers use a machine called a radar to see where planes are in the air.

SECURITY SEEK

PEOPLE AND BAGS ARE CHECKED CAREFULLY AT SECURITY. CAN YOU SPOT THE ITEMS BELOW IN THE PICTURE? CHECK THEM OFF AS YOU GO.

- [ ] HAND SCANNER
- [ ] GREEN CAP
- [ ] SLEEPING BABY
- [ ] GLOBE STICKER
- [ ] TWO RED LIGHTS
- [ ] THREE YELLOW ARROWS

GATES 1-10

Airport X-ray scanners can detect everything from metals to paper to liquid.

TWO MUSTACHES

BLUE BOOTS

GRAY BEARD

NECK SCARF

MOBILE PHONE

THREE PAIRS OF GLASSES

COUNTRY MAYHEM

SOME LETTERS HAVE GONE MISSING FROM THESE COUNTRY NAMES!
CAN YOU FILL IN THE BLANKS USING THE MISSING LETTERS BELOW?

 1. C A _ _ D A

 2. G R _ _ C E

 3. A R G _ _ T I N A

 4. C H _ _ E

 5. J A _ _ N

 6. F I _ _

MISSING LETTERS

(E N)   (J I)   (N A)   (I L)   (E E)   (P A)

WINGING IT

FILL IN THE GRID SO THAT EACH ROW, COLUMN, AND
SECTION CONTAINS ALL THE LETTERS IN THE WORD "WING."

W	I		G
		W	
I			W
	W	I	

A biplane is an aircraft that has one wing above the other. Biplanes were invented in the early 1900s.

FLYING HIGH

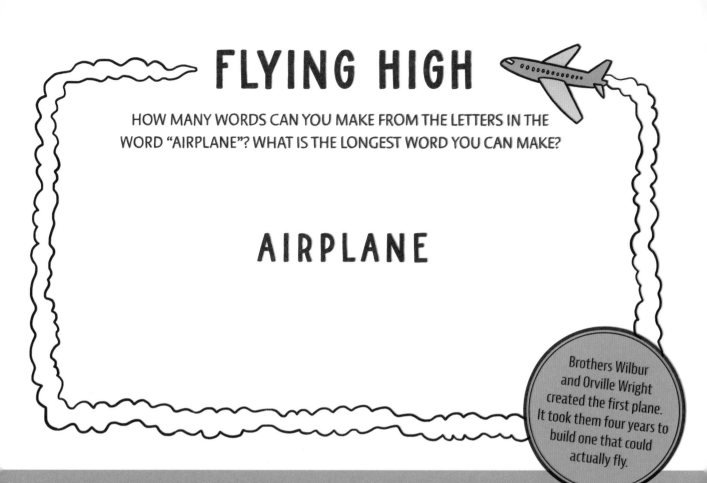

HOW MANY WORDS CAN YOU MAKE FROM THE LETTERS IN THE
WORD "AIRPLANE"? WHAT IS THE LONGEST WORD YOU CAN MAKE?

AIRPLANE

Brothers Wilbur
and Orville Wright
created the first plane.
It took them four years to
build one that could
actually fly.

FAMILY HOLIDAY

A FAMILY OF THREE IS FIGURING OUT WHERE TO SIT. USE THE CLUES TO HELP THEM.

CLUES

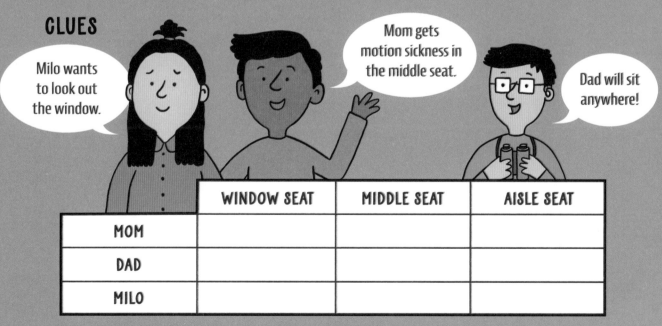

Milo wants
to look out
the window.

Mom gets
motion sickness in
the middle seat.

Dad will sit
anywhere!

	WINDOW SEAT	MIDDLE SEAT	AISLE SEAT
MOM			
DAD			
MILO			

Mark your answers on the grid with a check mark for the correct seat.
Rule out anywhere the family members can't sit with an "X."

AIRPORT JUMBLE

UNSCRAMBLE THESE WORDS TO DISCOVER DIFFERENT AREAS IN AN AIRPORT. USE THE CLUES TO HELP YOU.

1. The desk where passengers can collect their boarding pass in person.

KHCCE-NI

☐☐☐☐☐ – ☐☐

2. The area where passengers and bags are checked before they go on a plane.

YEUSCITR

☐☐☐☐☐☐☐☐

3. A large building where planes are stored or repaired.

HAGARN

☐☐☐☐☐☐

4. A place to have a sit-down meal while waiting for a flight.

UEARSTARTN

☐☐☐☐☐☐☐☐☐☐

5. The area where passports and boarding passes are checked before boarding a plane.

EGTA

☐☐☐☐

6. The area that planes take off from.

UYANRW

☐☐☐☐☐☐

TRAVELING AFTER LANDING

SOLVE THE CLUES AND FILL IN THE CROSSWORD.

ACROSS
1. A large motor vehicle that carries lots of passengers by road
3. A two-wheeled motor vehicle
5. A car that can be hired to take passengers somewhere
6. To travel on foot

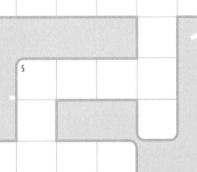

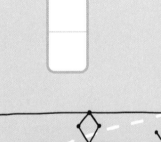

DOWN
1. A vessel for traveling by water
2. A series of carriages that move along tracks
4. A road vehicle with four wheels, for a small number of passengers
5. A type of train that travels along rails on streets, mainly in cities

The first taxi was actually a horse-drawn carriage.

TIC-TRAIL-TOE

TAKE TURNS DRAWING AN "X" OR AN "O" IN THE VAPOR TRAIL GRIDS. WHO CAN GET THREE IN A ROW FIRST? LINES CAN GO HORIZONTALLY, VERTICALLY, OR DIAGONALLY.

The white streaks that a plane leaves behind in the sky are called contrails. They are made of water.

CASE-DOKU

FILL IN THE GRID SO THAT EACH ROW, COLUMN, AND SECTION CONTAINS ALL THE LETTERS OF THE WORD "CASE."

C	A		E
		C	
A			C
	C		

CRISS-CROSS CAPITALS

PLACE THESE CAPITAL CITIES IN THE GRID.
LOOK CAREFULLY AT THE NUMBER
OF LETTERS TO HELP YOU.

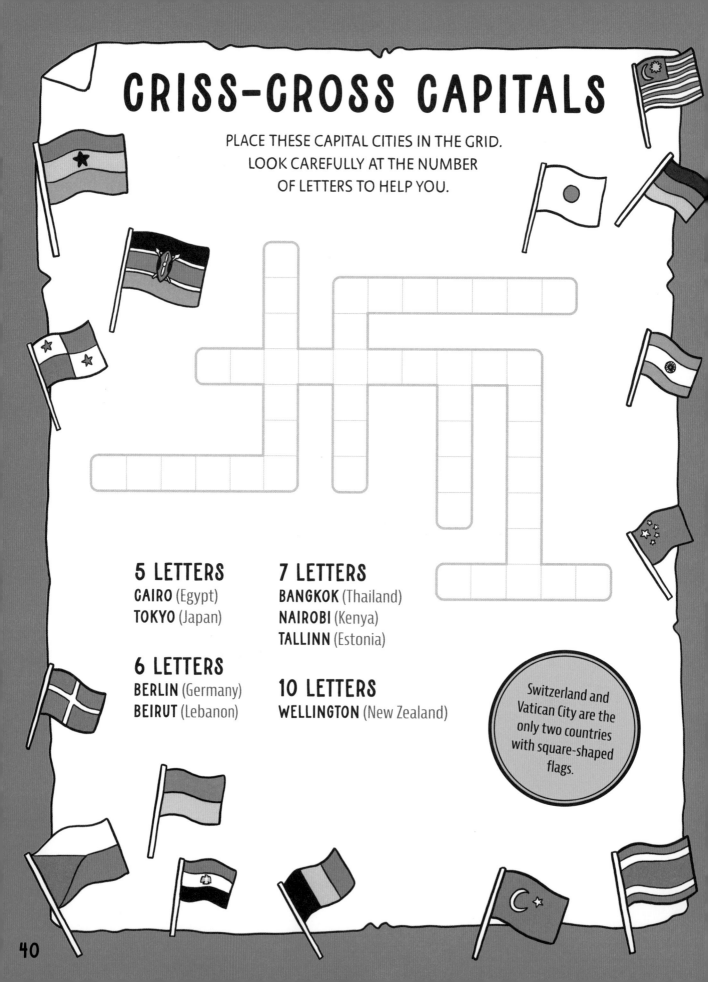

5 LETTERS
CAIRO (Egypt)
TOKYO (Japan)

6 LETTERS
BERLIN (Germany)
BEIRUT (Lebanon)

7 LETTERS
BANGKOK (Thailand)
NAIROBI (Kenya)
TALLINN (Estonia)

10 LETTERS
WELLINGTON (New Zealand)

Switzerland and Vatican City are the only two countries with square-shaped flags.

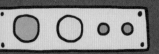

X-RAY VISION

LOOK CLOSELY AT THIS X-RAY OF A SUITCASE. WHAT DO YOU SEE INSIDE? TRY TO REMEMBER AS MUCH AS YOU CAN, THEN TURN THE PAGE TO TEST YOUR MEMORY.

Diamonds do not show up on X-ray machines.

X-RAY VISION

THINK BACK TO THE PICTURE OF THE
SUITCASE X-RAY ON THE PREVIOUS PAGE.
CAN YOU ANSWER ALL THESE QUESTIONS?

2
Did the passenger
pack sunglasses?

_____

1
How many pairs of
socks were in the suitcase?

_____

3
What number was on
the bottle of sunscreen?

_____

5
How many items in
the suitcase had a cable?

_____

4
Did the passenger
remember their toothbrush?

_____

6
What type of hat
did the passenger pack?

_____

7
Which two items can the
passenger take photos with?

_____

BIPLANE POWER

COLOR IN THIS PICTURE USING THE KEY.

1 = YELLOW   2 = RED   3 = GREEN   4 = GREY   5 = BROWN   6 = BLUE

AIRPLANE ART

FOLLOW THE STEPS TO DRAW YOUR OWN PASSENGER PLANE.

1 Draw a long sausage shape, with a straight diagonal line on the right end, as shown.

2 Draw a tail fin shape above the right end of the sausage.

3 Draw diagonal lines to make a slanted rectangle shape. This will be a wing.

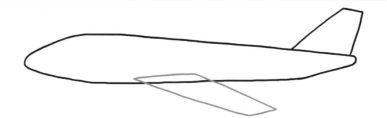

4 Create a similar shape below the tail fin to make a tail wing, as shown.

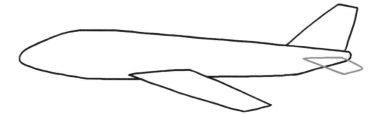

5 Draw diagonal lines to create a wing on the other side.

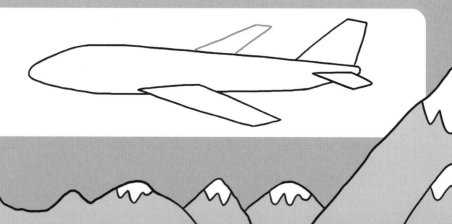

6 Draw two ovals below the first wing you drew. Connect these to the wing with curved lines to make two engines.

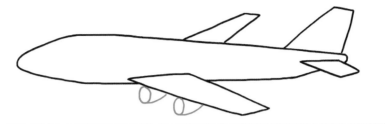

7 Draw a door at each end of the plane. Draw small windows along the side of the plane and at the front for the windshield, as shown.

8 Add extra details to decorate your plane, along with "whoosh" lines and clouds in the sky to give the illusion that your plane is flying.

9 Color your airplane to bring it to life!

NAME GAME

HOW WELL DO YOU KNOW AIR TRAVEL TRIVIA?
CIRCLE THE CORRECT ANSWER TO EACH
OF THESE QUESTIONS.

The first ever airplane flight only lasted 12 seconds.

1. The very first aircraft were not planes but balloons! Who made the first flying balloon?

THE MONTGOLFIER BROTHERS or **THE HILLIER SISTERS?**

2. What was the name of the airliner that could fly faster than the speed of sound?

SOUNDBOOM or **CONCORDE?**

3. Which ocean did Amelia Earhart fly solo over?

ARCTIC or **ATLANTIC?**

4. What was the name of the first person to build a real flying glider?

GEORGE BAILEY or **GEORGE CAYLEY?**

5. What do you call a plane that can take off from and land on water?

SEAPLANE or **AQUAPLANE?**

6. What was the relationship of Orville and Wilbur Wright, who made the first successful airplane flight?

BROTHERS or **COUSINS?**

PLANE BRAIN PUZZLES

CAN YOU FIGURE OUT THESE RIDDLES?

HOW OLD?

Two brothers flew to Hawaii twice. The first time they went, the youngest brother was four years old, and the oldest brother was twice his age.

The second time they went, the youngest brother was 12 years old.
How old was the oldest brother?

_____

AIR TRAFFIC CONTROL

The air traffic controller must manage three planes arriving at the same time.
Use the clues below to figure out where each plane should land.

· Plane A can only land on the red runway.
· Plane B can land on the blue or green runway.
· Plane C cannot land on the blue runway.

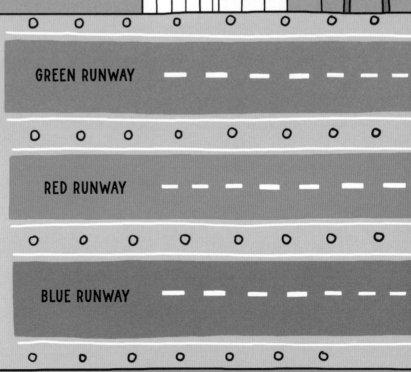

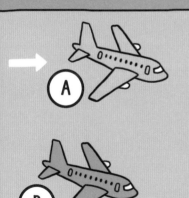

GREEN RUNWAY

RED RUNWAY

BLUE RUNWAY

UP IN THE AIR

CAN YOU FIND ALL THE WORDS IN THE GRID?

```
Y U S K C A N S T E W Q C S
O P K L X C V B N A T I X E
F D A S G H R E S R W M V C
J W I S H Z L C O J X R G H
T I S R S U R L Y N L M E R
E N L B N E L O P U I T V B
L D E Y E E N W G H S L D T
I O K N Y J W G T B N E U I
O W D R T N A M E R O B Y P
T R C O X G O N H R P T O K
S F L L E P I X O M Y A P C
G I T I M V C O B R L E M O
P Z M N D R D K T A E S B C
C S U I T C A S E K J N G E
```

AISLE

COCKPIT

DOOR

EXIT

LUGGAGE

PASSENGER

PILOT

SCREEN

SEAT

SEATBELT

SNACKS

SUITCASE

TOILET

TROLLEY

WINDOW

Airplanes fly about 35,000 feet (10,500 m) in the air. That's more than six miles above the ground!

PLANE JAM

LOOK CAREFULLY AT THIS BUSY SKY. HOW MANY
OF EACH FLYING OBJECT CAN YOU COUNT?

Unlike planes,
helicopters take off
and land vertically
(straight up and
down).

PASSENGER PLANES _____

BIPLANES _____

HELICOPTERS _____

HOT-AIR BALLOONS _____

PLAYING GAMES

FIND A FRIEND OR FAMILY MEMBER AND
PLAY THIS GAME TOGETHER.

Using a pen or pencil, take turns
connecting two side-by-side dots
horizontally or vertically (not
diagonally). When you complete a
full square, write your initial in the
box and take another turn.

C

Planes that perform aerobatics often spin and fly upside-down as part of their tricks.

As you play, think about how you can keep your opponent from making squares. When the entire grid is full of completed squares, count your initialled boxes.

The person with the most completed squares wins!

OUT OF THE WINDOW

WHAT CAN YOU SEE FROM THE WINDOW AS THE AIRPLANE TAKES OFF? DRAW IT HERE.

An airplane's window has three layers, or panels. The middle layer has a tiny hole in it that helps balance the air pressure in the cabin.

MONEY MATTERS

LOOK AT THESE CURRENCIES FROM AROUND THE WORLD.
CAN YOU FIT ALL THE WORDS INTO THE GRID?

The currency (money) used in Russia is called the ruble. In Mexico they use the peso. Seven other countries use pesos too!

3 LETTERS
WON

4 LETTERS
DRAM
PESO

5 LETTERS
DINAR
RUBLE

6 LETTERS
DOLLAR
KWANZA

8 LETTERS
STERLING

PLANE POETRY

WRITE AN ACROSTIC POEM ABOUT HOW IT FEELS TO FLY IN AN AIRPLANE.
USE THE LETTERS OF THE WORD "FLYING" TO START EACH LINE.

The first airmail was delivered by air balloon in 1859. Long ago, pigeons were used to send letters over long distances!

F _____

L _____

Y _____

I _____

N _____

G _____

MESSAGE IN THE SKY

USE THE CODE TO READ THE MESSAGE ON THE BANNER.

A B D E F

G H I L N

S T V W Y

The first non-stop, around-the-world flight took place in 1949. It took 94 hours.

_ _ _   _ _ _ _

_ _ _   _ _ _ _ _

BAGGAGE BARRIERS

HELP THIS SUITCASE FIND ITS WAY TO THE BAGGAGE HANDLERS AND ONTO THE PLANE. COLLECT THE SIX MISSING ITEMS ALONG THE WAY.

START

FINISH

STRAIGHT UP

CONNECT THE DOTS TO DISCOVER ANOTHER TYPE OF FLYING MACHINE.

BIG NAMES

The first hot-air balloon flight took place in 1783. The passengers were a duck, a sheep, and a rooster!

LOOK AT THIS LIST OF FAMOUS NAMES IN AIR TRAVEL HISTORY. CAN YOU FIT THE WORDS IN BOLD INTO THE GRID?

HINT: START WITH THE LONGEST WORD!

4 LETTERS

OTTO Lilienthal:
Builder of small early gliders, who made about 2,000 successful flights

Wiley **POST**:
The first person to fly solo all the way around the world

5 LETTERS

LOUIS Blériot:
Made the first powered flight across the English Channel

6 LETTERS

AMELIA Earhart:
The first woman to fly solo across the Atlantic

GEORGE Cayley:
Builder of the world's first glider

7 LETTERS

CHARLES Lindbergh:
The first person to cross the Atlantic in a plane without making any stops

Amy **JOHNSON**:
Flew by herself from England to Australia in 1930

11 LETTERS

Joseph and Étienne
MONTGOLFIER:
Builders of an early hot-air balloon that was the first to carry animals in the air

DREAM DESIGN

DESIGN A NEW LOOK FOR THIS AIRPLANE.
WHAT COLORS AND PATTERNS WILL YOU USE?

Airplane fuel
is stored in tanks
away from an airport.
It is transported to
the airport using
underground pipes.

CITY MYSTERY

CAN YOU THINK OF A CITY FOR EVERY LETTER OF THE ALPHABET? FILL THEM IN HERE.

Austin

B

C

D

E

F

G

H

I

J

K

L

M

N

O

P

Q

R

S

T

U

V

W

X

Y

Z

DESTINATION MUDDLE

UNSCRAMBLE THESE WORDS TO DISCOVER DIFFERENT PLACES YOU COULD GO BY PLANE. USE THE CLUES ABOVE THE PICTURES TO HELP YOU.

A large town to explore

1 IYTC
_____

An area of land surrounded by water

2 LINASD
_____

An area of large hills, sometimes snowy

3 OTSANUMIN
_____

A strip of sandy land by the water

4 HEBCA
_____

A tropical forest full of life

5 IFTOANRRSE
_____

A dry land, usually sandy

6 ETRDSE
_____

Not all deserts are hot. Some are cold. Antarctica is the largest desert in the world!

63

FLYING MACHINES

CAN YOU FIND ALL THE WORDS IN THE GRID?

```
W E M L K H G F D R O N E B
H P I H S R I A K E M E B V
E R C S D F J G N D F N G E
L A R T S G C A V B N A M N
I E O M U I L R E D I L G A
C N L P O P E R T U Y P N L
O A I G I N H L H G R A A P
P L G B R T O H B N C E I O
T P H A R H G P F D S S R G
E T T L T Y S D L G B J L R
R N N L M F C V M A H K I A
W U X O E Y J M C R N W N C
V T R O C K E T M V B E E H
Y S R N F G T B I R X S R L
```

AIRLINER	BIPLANE	GLIDER	MICROLIGHT	SEAPLANE
AIRSHIP	CARGO PLANE	HELICOPTER	MONOPLANE	STUNT PLANE
BALLOON	DRONE	JET	ROCKET	

A floatplane is a type of seaplane that has special "floats" that allow it to take off from and land on water.

COCKPIT CODES

SOLVE THE PROBLEMS TO FIGURE OUT THE CODE.
THEN ANSWER THE QUESTION BELOW.

The first female pilot was Raymonde de Laroche of France. She earned her pilot's licence in 1910.

(A) 8 + 8 = ___   (E) 20 − 5 = ___   (M) 19 − 10 = ___

(B) 15 − 3 = ___   (K) 11 + 7 = ___   (O) 10 − 10 = ___

(C) 13 − 10 = ___   (L) 6 + 7 = ___   (X) 2 + 5 = ___

What is the name of the device that records all the information from a flight?

12	13	16	3	18

12	0	7

WHERE IN THE WORLD?

SOME AMAZING LANDMARKS CAN BE FOUND AROUND THE WORLD. CAN YOU MATCH EACH TRAVEL TICKET TO THE LANDMARK THAT IS BEING VISITED?

DESTINATION: **DELHI INDIA** — 22/01 SEAT 11D — FLIGHT NO. NYT928

DESTINATION: **LONDON UK** — 17/04 SEAT 14C — FLIGHT NO. XB104

BIG BEN

EIFFEL TOWER

MACHU PICCHU

TABLE MOUNTAIN

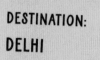

DESTINATION: **CAIRO EGYPT** — 26/11 SEAT 20E — FLIGHT NO. 87301

DESTINATION: **SAN FRANCISCO USA** — 23/02 SEAT 01F — FLIGHT NO. NF335

DESTINATION:
CAIRNS AUSTRALIA

28/08
SEAT 44B   FLIGHT NO. N8337

02/05
SEAT 46A   FLIGHT NO. 822D
DESTINATION: CAPE TOWN
SOUTH AFRICA

Egypt's Great Pyramid of Giza is the tallest pyramid in the world. It was the tallest structure on Earth for 4,000 years!

TAJ
MAHAL

GOLDEN GATE
BRIDGE

GREAT PYRAMID
OF GIZA

GREAT BARRIER REEF

DESTINATION: CUZCO PERU
28/12
SEAT 16C   FLIGHT NO. ZY398

DESTINATION: 01/07
PARIS   SEAT 15A
FRANCE   FLIGHT NO. 300YN

TIME TO DEPART

HOW MANY WORDS CAN YOU MAKE FROM THE LETTERS IN THE WORD "DEPARTURE"? WHAT'S THE LONGEST WORD YOU CAN MAKE?

DEPARTURE

The Concorde was a super-fast airplane. It could fly from London to New York in just 3.5 hours. Most planes take about 7.5 hours.

GATE GRID

FILL IN THE GRID SO THAT EACH ROW, COLUMN, AND SECTION CONTAINS ALL THE LETTERS OF THE WORD "GATE."

G			E
A		G	
		E	
E			G

AWESOME ADVERT

DESIGN A POSTER FOR A PLACE YOU CAN TRAVEL TO BY PLANE.
WHAT'S YOUR FAVORITE THING TO DO OR SEE? DRAW IT HERE.

ON THE JOB

SOLVE THE CLUES AND FILL IN THE CROSSWORD.

The Isle of Barra, Scotland, has one of the world's smallest airports. The runway is the island's beach!

ACROSS

2. _ _ _ _ _ _ _ _ staff keep the airport and passengers safe and secure
4. This worker repairs and maintains airplanes and helicopters
5. The person who flies the plane
6. An air _ _ _ _ _ _ _ controller speaks to the pilot during the flight

DOWN

1. On the plane, flight _ _ _ _ _ _ _ _ _ _ keep passengers comfortable
3. A person who sorts luggage at the airport is a baggage _ _ _ _ _ _ _
7. Before a flight, ground _ _ _ _ check that the plane is working properly

TRAVELING TICKLES

DRAW LINES TO MATCH EACH JOKE TO ITS PUNCHLINE.

At Denver airport in Colorado, USA, there is a special baggage carousel just for skis and snowboards.

1 Where do wasps go on their holidays?

2 What did one volcano say to the other volcano?

3 Where do songbirds go on holiday?

4 What kind of chocolate is sold in an airport gift shop?

5 What did one ocean say to the other ocean?

A "I lava you!"

B Nothing. It just waved!

C Sting-apore!

D Plane chocolate!

E The Canary Isles!

BORN FOR ADVENTURE

WRITE AN ACROSTIC POEM ABOUT GOING ON ADVENTURES.
USE THE LETTERS IN THE WORD "ADVENTURE" BELOW TO START EACH LINE.

A _____

D _____

V _____

E _____

N _____

T _____

U _____

R _____

E _____

The first flight over the South Pole happened in 1929. The flight lasted about 19 hours.

BAGGAGE CLAIM

FOLLOW THE LINES TO HELP EACH PASSENGER FIND THEIR LUGGAGE.

The word 'luggage' was first used in the late 1500s.

ARE WE THERE YET?

CAN YOU SPOT ALL THE ITEMS BELOW THROUGH THE WINDOWS AS THE PLANE COMES IN TO LAND? CHECK THEM OFF AS YOU GO.

☐ SANDCASTLE

☐ CIRCUS TENT

☐ BEACH UMBRELLA

☐ WHITE SURFBOARD

☐ BLUE SKYSCRAPER

☐ LIGHTHOUSE

When landing at Reagan National Airport, you can see wide views of many landmarks in the U.S. capital, Washington, D.C.

SEVEN SHELLS

YELLOW BUS

DOLPHIN

ORANGE FLAG

CRAB

LIFE JACKET

SUPER SKETCH

FOLLOW THE STEPS TO DRAW YOUR OWN PROPELLER PLANE.

Draw a large oval with a point on one end. This is the main body of your propeller plane.

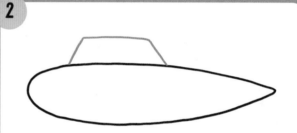

Draw a rectangle with slanted sides on top of the oval shape, as shown, to make a cockpit.

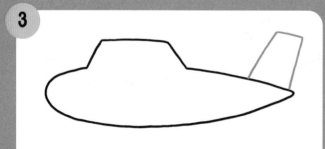

Give your plane a tail by drawing a tall slanted rectangle shape on top of the pointed end of the oval.

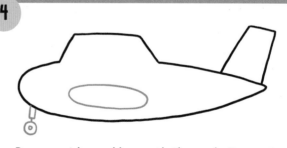

Draw a wide oval beneath the cockpit area to create a wing. Sketch a little rectangle below the front of the plane and add two small circles to the bottom of it to make a wheel.

5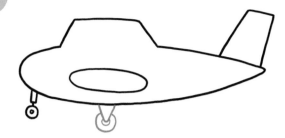

At the lowest point of the oval shape, roughly in the middle, draw a triangle. Draw two circles behind it to create a second wheel.

6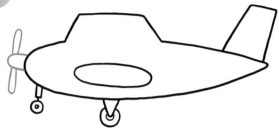

Add the propeller to the front of your plane, as shown.

7

Draw a small square in the middle of the cockpit. Then draw squares with slanted edges on either side of the middle one. These are the windows.

8

Decorate the plane and draw lines around the outside to make it look like it's moving.

9

Color your plane with your favorite felt-tip pens or pencils.

AIRPORT ARRIVALS

FAMILY AND FRIENDS ARE WAITING EXCITEDLY FOR PASSENGERS TO ARRIVE.
FIT THESE ITEMS FROM ARRIVALS INTO THE GRID.

3 LETTERS
HUG

4 LETTERS
BAGS
KISS

5 LETTERS
GIFTS

6 LETTERS
BANNER
SMILES

7 LETTERS
BARRIER
FLOWERS

PILOTS AT WORK

LOOK CLOSELY AT THIS PICTURE OF THE COCKPIT. WHAT CAN YOU SPOT?
TRY TO REMEMBER AS MANY DETAILS AS YOU CAN,
THEN TURN THE PAGE TO TEST YOUR MEMORY.

A plane's cockpit is packed with flight instruments that tell the pilots the information they need to fly the plane.

PILOTS AT WORK

THINK BACK TO THE PICTURE OF THE COCKPIT ON THE PREVIOUS PAGE.
CAN YOU ANSWER QUESTIONS BELOW?

1
How many pilots
were flying the plane?

_____

2
What color was
the hot-air balloon?

_____

3
How many
boats were there?

_____

5
How many radar
screens were there?

_____

4
Was the plane flying
over land or water?

_____

6
What color was the
pilot's watch?

_____

7
Were either of the
pilots wearing glasses?

_____

8
What color
were the chairs?

_____

IN THE BUILDING

HOW MANY WORDS CAN YOU MAKE FROM THE LETTERS IN THE WORD "TERMINAL"? WHAT'S THE LONGEST WORD YOU CAN MAKE?

TERMINAL

An airport terminal is the main building that passengers go to, either to catch a plane or get their luggage once they have landed.

SUDOKU CHALLENGE

FILL IN THE GRID SO THAT EACH ROW, COLUMN, AND SECTION CONTAINS ALL THE LETTERS OF THE WORD "FLIGHT."

F	L	I	G	H	T
	G				F
		F	H		
H	T	L		G	I
I	F		T		H
	H		I	F	G

SKY-HIGH SKETCH

FILL THIS SKY WITH THINGS THAT FLY.
HOW MANY CAN YOU THINK OF?

82

HOLIDAY SHOPPING

London and New York are tied for having the most airports in one city. They both have six!

UNSCRAMBLE THE WORDS TO UNCOVER ITEMS THAT YOU MIGHT BUY ON VACATION. USE THE CLUES TO HELP YOU.

A special item to remember a trip

1 VRSEONUI

_____

A lotion to protect skin from the Sun

2 NSU ARCEM

_____

A chilly treat to eat

3 CEI MERCA

_____

Clothes to wear on your legs

4 SROSHT

_____

An item worn to protect your eyes

5 NSASLUGSES

_____

Something to wear on your head

6 AHT

_____

SUITCASE SPOT

FIND AND CIRCLE THE 10 DIFFERENCES
BETWEEN THESE TWO OPEN SUITCASES.

If you ever visit
Mawsynram, India,
pack an umbrella.
It is the rainiest place
in the world!

FINAL PREPARATIONS

CAN YOU SPOT THESE ITEMS AS THE WORKERS GET THE PLANE READY FOR TRAVEL? CHECK THEM OFF AS YOU GO.

- [ ] AIR TRAFFIC CONTROL TOWER
- [ ] FIVE TRAFFIC CONES
- [ ] FUEL HOSE
- [ ] FOX
- [ ] FIRE ENGINE
- [ ] THREE FLAGS

- [ ] SPOTTY SUITCASE
- [ ] TWO YELLOW HELMETS
- [ ] GREEN AIRPLANE
- [ ] BLUE BIRD
- [ ] BUS
- [ ] FIVE LEAVES

King Fahd International Airport in Saudi Arabia is the largest airport in the world. If it was placed in London, UK, it would take up almost half the city!

FLY THE FLAG

IMAGINE YOU DISCOVERED A BRAND NEW COUNTRY.
DESIGN ITS FLAG HERE. WHAT WOULD YOU NAME IT?

Red is the most common colour on country flags.

My country's name:

PLANE POWER

CAN YOU FIND ALL THE WORDS IN THE GRID?

Runways have strips of lights to help guide planes during takeoff and landing.

```
W L M B R W I N G S P A N V
S E L O U D X O B K C A L B
Y C P I N U E S D F G L A C
T O H D W R H S J K R T N C
I N H F A G C M C B N D D A
V T W T Y A S D F E H O I V
A R Y U A I O P D L N F N I
R O G F X P J U N R H T G G
G L M R L U T M V B A M G A
R T W O C I M H C G H G E T
Q O V B T N F Y G O P I A O
C W V L R O T T A I L V R R
U E A I C N R N Y U L B K R
V R E F R A D I O D G F H T
```

ALTITUDE	DESCENT	GRAVITY	MOTOR	RUNWAY
BLACK BOX	DRAG	LANDING GEAR	NAVIGATOR	TAIL
CONTROL TOWER	FLIGHT PATH	LIFT	RADIO	WINGSPAN

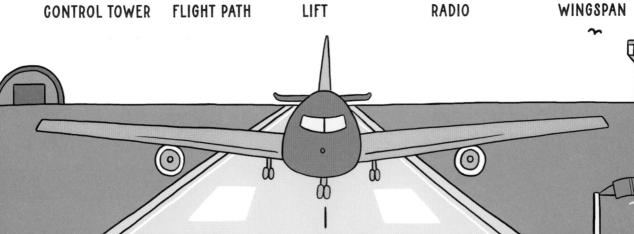

89

LOADS OF LAUGHS

DRAW LINES TO MATCH EACH JOKE TO ITS PUNCHLINE.

1. Why do robots go on vacation?

2. Why don't mummies ever go on vacation?

3. What did the alpaca say when the llama suggested they go on vacation?

4. What do you call a plane that can't take off?

5. What is black, white and red all over?

A. A penguin with sunburn!

B. An error-plane!

C. "Alpaca my bags!"

D. They don't want to unwind!

E. To recharge their batteries!

VACATION WORDPLAY

SOLVE THE CLUES AND FILL IN THE CROSSWORD.

ACROSS
3. A place to stay on vacation, with extra activities and things to do
5. A vacation taken on a large passenger ship
6. To plan a vacation, you might visit a travel _ _ _ _ _
7. People in _ _ _ _ _ class on an airplane get luxury service
8. You need this in the right currency to buy things on vacation

Spain is the second-most visited country in the world after France.

DOWN
1. A large building that people sleep in when they are away from home
2. What you might call a vacation spent at home
4. You take _ _ _ _ _ _ with a camera to remember special moments

GONE MISSING

SOME LETTERS FROM THESE MAJOR CITIES HAVE GONE MISSING! CAN YOU FILL IN THE BLANKS USING THE MISSING LETTERS BELOW?

The world's largest tropical island is New Guinea, located just north of Australia.

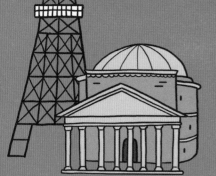

1. C _ _ R O   2. D _ _ H I   3. T O K _ _

4. R O _ _   5. D A _ _ A S   6. M E L B _ _ R N E

ME   **EL**   **AI**

OU   **YO**   **LL**

RIDDLE ME THIS

CAN YOU SOLVE THIS TRICKY TRAVEL QUESTION?

A family has four suitcases. The red suitcase is heavier than the blue suitcase, but lighter than the green suitcase. The yellow suitcase is lighter than the blue suitcase.

Which suitcase is the heaviest of all?

_____

SPECIAL SOUVENIR

HOW MANY WORDS CAN YOU MAKE FROM THE LETTERS IN THE WORD 'SOUVENIR'? WHAT'S THE LONGEST WORD YOU CAN MAKE?

SOUVENIR

SUDOKU CHALLENGE

FILL IN THE GRID SO THAT EACH ROW, COLUMN, AND SECTION CONTAINS ALL THE LETTERS OF THE WORD "RUNWAY."

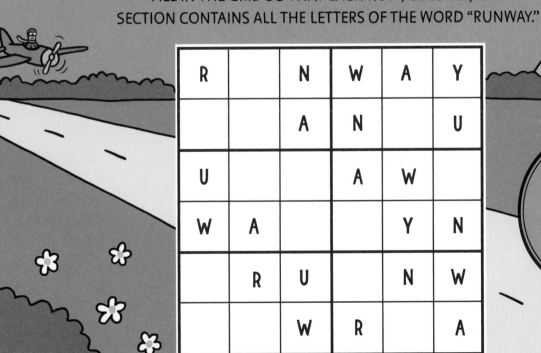

R	N	W	A	Y	
	A	N			U
U		A	W		
W	A			Y	N
	R	U		N	W
	W	R		A	

Some military planes can refuel while they are flying. Special refueling jets connect to the aircraft using a hose.

ANSWERS

p2

```
        S
        U           T
   P    I        T  A     T
  A I R P O R T   I  L     I
  I     C          C       C
  L     A         P A S S P O R T
  O     S          E       E
  T    W I N G     T  R    T
                      U
                   G A T E
                      N
                      W
                      A
                      Y
```

p3

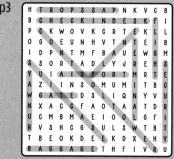

p5 Airplane 4

p6

```
        B
        O
M A G A Z I N E
        A
H E A D P H O N E S
        D
S A N I T I S E R
        I
        N P A S S P O R T
        G   S   U
        P   U   N
        A   N   G
        S   G   L
        S   L   A
            A   S
            S W A T E R
            S   S
              T R A V E L P I L L O W
                  S
```

p7 Airplane 3

p8-9

p12-13

p14 Olá – Portuguese
Ciao – Italian
Hallo – Dutch
Nǐ hǎo – Chinese
Namaste – Hindi
Bonjour – French

p16

B	I	R	D
R	D	B	I
I	R	D	B
D	B	I	R

L	D	A	N
N	A	L	D
A	N	D	L
D	L	N	A

p17 1-D, 2-A, 3-E, 4-B, 5-C

p19 NOW BOARDING

p20-21
The flight from Perth to Tokyo is one-way only.

p22

p23 HAVE A GOOD FLIGHT!

p26-27
1. Yes, she has landed, 2. Shanghai,
3. Yes, she will make it, 4. Paris,
5. Istanbul, 6. 17, 7. Gate 3,
8. Boston

p28

p29

p30 1. ENGINE, 2. WINGS, 3. NOSE,
4. TAIL, 5. HOLD

p32-33

p34 1. CANADA, 2. GREECE,
3. ARGENTINA, 4. CHILE,
5. JAPAN, 6. FIJI

W	I	N	G
N	G	W	I
I	N	G	W
G	W	I	N

p35 Mom – Aisle seat
Dad – Middle seat
Milo – Window seat

p36 1. CHECK-IN, 2. SECURITY,
3. HANGAR, 4. RESTAURANT,
5. GATE, 6. RUNWAY

p37

Crossword:
BUS / BOAT / MOTORCYCLE / TRAIN / TAXI / CAR / TRAM / WALK

p39

C	A	S	E
S	E	C	A
A	S	E	C
E	C	A	S

p40

TALLINN / BEIRUT / BANGKOK / WELLINGTON / TOKYO / NAIROBI / BERLIN / CAIRO

p42 1. One pair, 2. Yes, 3. 50,
4. Yes, 5. Two items, 6. Cap,
7. Camera and phone

p46 1. The Montgolfier brothers,
2. Concorde, 3. Atlantic,
4. George Cayley, 5. Seaplane,
6. Brothers

p47 HOW OLD?
The oldest brother was 16
years old

AIR TRAFFIC CONTROL
Plane A - Red runway
Plane B - Blue runway
Plane C - Green runway

p48

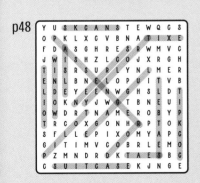

p49 PASSENGER PLANES: 5
BIPLANES: 9
HELICOPTERS: 7
HOT-AIR BALLOONS: 11

p53

PESO / STERLING / RUBLE / DINAR / DOLLAR / DRAM / KWANZA / WON

p55 FLY HIGH AND SHINE

p56-57

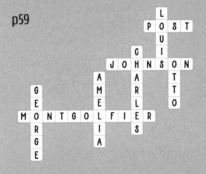

p59

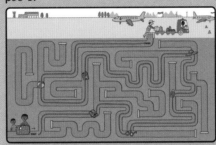

POST / LOUISON / JOHNSON / CHARLES / OTTO / AMELIA / GEORGE / MONTGOLFIER

p63 1. CITY, 2. ISLAND, 3. MOUNTAINS,
4. BEACH, 5. RAINFOREST, 6. DESERT

p64

p65 BLACK BOX

p66-67

Delhi, India – Taj Mahal
London, UK – Big Ben
Cairns, Australia –
    Great Barrier Reef
Cape Town, South Africa –
    Table Mountain
Cairo, Egypt – Great Pyramid of Giza
San Francisco, USA –
    Golden Gate Bridge
Cuzco, Peru – Machu Picchu
Paris, France – Eiffel Tower

p68

G	T	A	E
A	E	G	T
T	G	E	A
E	A	T	G

p70

SECURITY / ATTENDANTS / MECHANIC / HANDLER / PILOT / TRAFFIC / CREW

p71 1-C, 2-A, 3-E, 4-D, 5-B

p73 1-C, 2-D, 3-A, 4-B

p74-75

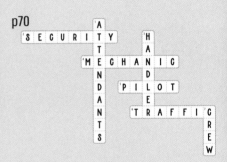

p78

KISS / BARRIER / BANNER / HUG / GIFT / BAG / FLOWERS / SMILES

p80 1. Two, 2. Red, 3. Four, 4. Water, 5. Two, 6. Green, 7. Yes, 8. Yellow

p81

F	L	I	G	H	T
T	G	H	L	I	F
G	I	F	H	T	L
H	T	L	F	G	I
I	F	G	T	L	H
L	H	T	I	F	G

p84 1. Souvenir, 2. Sunscreen, 3. Ice cream, 4. Shorts, 5. Sunglasses, 6. Hat

p85

p86-87

p88

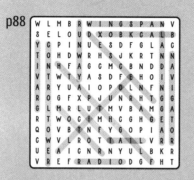

p90 1-E, 2-D, 3-C, 4-B, 5-A

p91

p92 1. CAIRO, 2. DELHI, 3. TOKYO, 4. ROME, 5. DALLAS, 6. MELBOURNE

RIDDLE ME THIS
The green suitcase is heaviest

p93

R	U	N	W	A	Y
Y	W	A	N	R	U
U	N	Y	A	W	R
W	A	R	U	Y	N
A	R	U	Y	N	W
N	Y	W	R	U	A

ACKNOWLEDGMENTS

Commissioned and project managed by Duck Egg Blue Limited

Author: Laura Baker
Editor: Priyanka Lamichhane
Illustrator: Sophie Foster
Designers: Andy Mansfield, Stephen Scanlan and Duck Egg Blue Limited
Publishing Director: Piers Pickard
Publisher: Rebecca Hunt
Art Director: Andy Mansfield
Print Production: Nigel Longuet

Published in May 2024 by Lonely Planet Global Limited
CRN: 554153
ISBN: 978 1 83758 296 9
www.lonelyplanet.com/kids
© Lonely Planet 2024

10 9 8 7 6 5 4 3 2 1

Printed in China

STAY IN TOUCH

lonelyplanet.com/contact

Lonely Planet Office:
IRELAND
Digital Depot, Roe Lane
(off Thomas St), Digital Hub,
Dublin 8, D08 TCV4, Ireland

MIX
Paper from responsible sources
FSC™ C021741

Paper in this book is certified against the Forest Stewardship Council™ standards. FSC™ promotes environmentally responsible, socially beneficial and economically viable management of the world's forests.